CAIRN TERRIERS

Among the most lovable and popular of all the Terrier family, the Cairn will always hold a special place in the hearts of dog-lovers. H. F. Whitehead, late Secretary of the Cairn Terrier Club, writes with infectious enthusiasm on all aspects of their care and breeding.

Frontispiece Ch. Oudenarde Midnight Chimes

CAIRN TERRIERS

BY

LT. COL. HECTOR F. WHITEHEAD, D.S.O.

Edited & Revised by
ANNE MACDONALD

FOYLES HANDBOOKS
LONDON

ISBN 0 7071 0573 0

© W. & G. Foyle 1959, 1976

First published 1959
6th impression 1970
Reprinted 1973
Revised Edition 1976

Published in Great Britain by
W. & G. Foyle Ltd.,
125 Charing Cross Road,
London, WC2H 0EB

Dedication

*In memory of my wife who loved
Cairns so sincerely, and whose wish
was that this book should be written
and published some day*

H. F. Whitehead.

*Photoset, printed and bound
in Great Britain by*
REDWOOD BURN LIMITED
Trowbridge & Esher

CONTENTS

LIST OF ILLUSTRATIONS

FOREWORD

When my old Friend, Hector Whitehead, asked that I should write a foreword to this book on the Cairn Terrier, it gave me great pleasure. Not having been in the 'Dog Show World' for a long time, I think it might be better if I went back over the years—perhaps more than is pleasant to contemplate. The Cairn has worked his way into the hearts of many, all over the world literally, including royalty—the Duke of Windsor owned several, when he was Prince of Wales. There are also representatives in the Island of Kerguelen, for instance.

The Cairn is now firmly established with the general public, and very well known for his charming and individualistic character, although he is now, naturally, much more level in type than 40 or 50 years ago. For the benefit of present-day owners, I draw on my memory of over 40 years, when I knew at first hand the working terriers of those days, known under various local names, such as Glenalladale, etc.

My first Cairn was one of the many working terriers owning no breed name and to be found in the North, along the North-west Coast of Scotland, and all the Inner and Outer Isles—the Hebrides. It was in 1908, during a shooting expedition in North Uist, that I acquired 'Lexie', a very small red-brindled bitch. I had her from a policeman in Lochmaddy, with one ear up, but the other only sometimes. My next Cairn, 'Teddy', came from a Lochshieldside stalker—a big dog by present-day standards, foxy-red with a light eye and liver-coloured nose. He would face anything that grew hair—otter, fox or badger, all were his delight to tackle.

To my mind, the old working Cairns were longer in the back and much more active than the 'cut-and-dried' modern type. There is a danger, I fear, of the present representatives of the breed becoming stiff movers, with poor hindquarters, and loss of agility.

No longer being required to work, there is the risk of their becoming different from what they were originally intended. But the Cairn has kept his original type in regard to colour, head and expression more than most breeds in recent years, and the show bench has not spoiled it yet. It lies with all Cairn lovers to see that this does not happen.

When Mrs Alastair Campbell, the first secretary of the Cairn Terrier Club and one of the prime movers in getting this gallant worker recognized by the Kennel Club, and named 'The Cairn Terrier', started breeding, they were all shapes and sizes. It was my privilege to succeed Mrs Campbell as secretary, and Hector Whitehead followed me in 1926. There never has been anyone who has put in more time and work on behalf of the Cairn in every way than the author, spreading the fame of this great little terrier far and wide. I feel sure that this book will be a further contribution to that end.

IAN EWING, *Major*,
Mounthooly, Jedburgh,
Roxburghshire

INTRODUCTION

EVER SINCE I first owned a dog, I wondered how he had come to be the friend of man, with all the love and devotion he displays. It was evident that someone had plucked him from the wild, and if ever a monument was worth raising, it was to the man or woman who had done this in the long past years. How it was done was clearly demonstrated, in my view, by two arrivals some years ago, at the Royal Zoological Park at Edinburgh. These were two beautiful tigers, as easy to handle as a St Bernard and very like them except that they were not so tall. In the Malayan Peninsula, a tigress was shot and her den found with four very young cubs. They were to be destroyed, too, but the planter's wife intervened and thought that they could be reared. One died but the other three were reared successfully and ultimately two came to Edinburgh. This might well have happened ages ago and through the kind-heartedness of woman, the ancestor of our dog was spared, to our immeasurable benefit now.

All breeds have their staunch upholders, who see and appreciate the good points. Practically every breed differs from the others in some respects, but even within each breed, every dog is an individual. The most individualistic breed is the Cairn Terrier, the name granted to the little fellow by the Kennel Club, although he has existed in the Highlands and Islands of Scotland since time immemorial. He is now one of the leading Terriers in Britain when it comes to the number of registrations with the Kennel Club or the number of Terriers at any Championship show—a position he occupies purely on his merits as a companionable, amenable and loyal little pal, yet with that spark of mischief that makes him so lovable. No tame sheep to suffer injustice, and willing to stand up to anything once thoroughly aroused. He may be any colour, but not black and not white, as the former colour makes him look like his descendant the Scottish Terrier, while the latter colour would make him a West Highland White Terrier, though not a good specimen.

His original use was to hunt and kill foxes, otters and other 'vermin' in his native land, and even today he is used for this purpose although the quarry is not so prolific as in the old days.

His history goes back to the dim and distant past before the days when records were kept. The earliest notice is by Bishop Lesley of Ross who describes a 'dog of low height which, creeping into subterraneous burrows, routs out foxes, badgers, martins and wild cats from their lurking places and dens; and if he at any time finds the passage too narrow, opens himself a way with his feet, and that with so great labour that he frequently perishes through his own exertions'. This was in the 15th century. An interesting point arose with King James VI of Scotland and I of England, when he sent 'Terrars' to the King of France by ship, and thought them so valuable that a 'Ship of War' accompanied them to see that no harm arose. These were the small dogs that were used for clearing vermin, and they had to be stout of heart and hard as nails or they would not go into the holes in the rocks to find their natural prey. These dogs would not be so kindly treated as today, but they were the foundation of our Scottish breeds. As shows became popular after 1860, more interest was shown in the varieties of dogs and they became classified, and the results gave rise to much acrimony. The first dog of Scotland was the Skye Terrier, and then the Scotch Terrier, though the latter had more of Yorkshire Terrier appearance at the first shows.

Then came the West Highland White Terrier, although there were also White Scottish Terriers. This brings us down to the years after the South African War, and it was felt by many Highlanders that it was time the original dog was given some say in the dog world. So there was registered with the Kennel Club a dog called the 'Short-haired Skye', and he was shown as such, with the first class at any show being at Inverness in 1909. Immediately a most acrimonious dispute arose over the name, and the Skye Terrier enthusiasts whose dog has a coat of some 5 inches long, would have none of it and appealed to the Kennel Club. Finally the name Cairn Terrier was given to 'The best little Pal in the World'. It is strange that the name might have been given to the Scottish Terrier, as we know him now, for Mr Thomson Gray in his *Dogs of Scotland*, 1891, says 'The terrier which we now recognize as the Scottish Terrier is the hard-haired Highland or Cairn Terrier, known in the Highland glens as the "fox" terrier, and in Skye as the pure Skye Terrier.' Fortunately that was not the case. To bear out the above, I remember as a boy that the smooth fox terrier, as we know him now, was called in the North of Scotland 'the English Fox-Terrier' thus presuming that there was a local fox terrier.

The Highland proprietors and lairds had their own packs and each was bred and kept purely for pluck and fighting capacity, and appearance or points did not come into the picture, but once they ventured on the show bench this regulation of type had to be gone into and a meeting was held in Edinburgh in 1910, where a standard was drawn up and will be discussed in a later chapter. Amongst those at that meeting were the chief protagonists of the breed, the Secretary, Mrs Alastair Campbell, the Hon. Mary Hawke, Lady Sophie Scott, Lady Charles Bentinck, with Mrs F. M. Ross, the breed historian, all now departed, and Mrs Fleming one of the most successful breeders. Few thought the Cairn would last, least of all that he would get to the top in some thirty years, but by sheer merit he made his way, without grooming or polishing—he walks straight into your heart—and no other breed will ever replace him. He should impress with his fearless and gay disposition—and he does.

In 1912, the registrations at the Kennel Club numbered almost 150, while in 1957 the total was 2,628, and in 1972 the registrations reached the enormous figure of 3,493.

Ch. Brucairn Red Robin who was B.O.B., Crufts 1969

CHAPTER ONE

WHAT IS A CAIRN?

IT IS OFTEN said at the ringside that Cairns appear to be of different types, but a lot of this is caused through the variety of colours and shades that can come between black and white. Never let the colour take your attention away from the formation of the dog. The Standard of Points accentuates from start to finish that the Cairn is not a mass of fads, nor is he otherwise than 'average' in everything—except pluck and lovableness.

CHARACTERISTICS. This terrier should impress with his fearless and gay disposition. Shyness or crossness is not a natural trait of the Cairn but it can be encouraged by bad rearing, or breeding from ancestors who had these traits. Both are difficult to eradicate in the adult dog.

APPEARANCE. Active, game, hardy, and 'shaggy' in appearance; strong, though compactly built. Should stand well forward on forepaws. Strong quarters, deep in ribs. Very free in movement. Coat hard enough to resist rain. Head small, but in proportion to body. A general foxy appearance is the chief characteristic of this working terrier.

Keep in view that the above brings in thirty per cent of the points at a show, and means that the dog should strike you as one who has a job, knows it, and carries it out, like a soldier who has been in action. Shaggy does not mean that the dog should be 'ragged' or unkempt, but with a fair coat and good head furnishings. The strong quarters enable him to force his way between rocks, and it would surprise you how narrow a slit he can squeeze into, and if not able to turn, he may have to be dug out. The term 'foxy' applies to appearance and not to head. Just as the expressions he fought like a tiger, noble as a lion, cunning as a serpent, have been used to characterize these particular beasts, so the Cairn approaches the fox more than any other animal—to be slangy and old time at that, he should look 'fly'. He had to beat the fox, but unfortunately a lot of that appearance has been lost through no work and all show.

HEAD AND SKULL. Skull broad in proportion; strong, but not too long or heavy jaw. A decided indentation between the eyes; hair should be full on forehead. Muzzle powerful but not heavy. Very strong jaw, which should be neither undershot nor overshot.

The skull is wedge-shaped and the length from nose to stop (the indentation referred to above) should be no longer than the length from stop to top of the head, occiput. While the forehead should be well covered, it should not have the amount of hair that is wanted on a Skye Terrier, where you have to part it to enable you to see the eyes and their colour. The dog is lightly built and so the head should not strike you as being big, indeed the dog should strike you as a whole, giving a well-proportioned, balanced appearance.

EYES. Set wide apart, medium in size, dark hazel, rather sunk, with shaggy eyebrows.

Here the word medium appears, and shows that there are two extremes, and though good for their own breed, not good for the Cairn. The small eye of the Smooth Fox Terrier would make him look mean and the large eye of the Pekingese soft and unterrier-like. Light eyes make him look vicious, and lack of good eyebrows makes him look 'plain'. Note the expression 'wide apart'.

EARS. Small, pointed, well carried and erect, but not too closely set. Breeders have practically eradicated 'bat' ears (round-pointed) and those set on the top of the head. Either or both of these take away from the expression very badly.

MOUTH. Large teeth. Jaw strong and level. When you consider that the Cairn has to tackle a fox much heavier than himself and that his bite must tell from the word 'go', you can understand the large teeth, and they should strike you as such compared with the size of the dog, and his head. Level jaws means that the bite may take the piece away with it, and are not merely for hanging on:

NECK. Well set on, but not too short. In other words it should fit into the conformation of the shoulders and body.

FOREQUARTERS. Sloping shoulder and a medium length of leg; good, but not too large, bone. Forelegs should not be out at elbow. Legs must be covered with hard hair.

This is very clear as he is a lightly built dog of great agility, and he should be well off-the-ground, and not low-to-ground like the Scottie.

BODY. Compact, straight back; well-sprung deep ribs; strong sinews; back medium in length and well coupled.

Here again you will note 'medium'. There should be no exaggerations, but his whole body in proportion, and noticeably so.

HINDQUARTERS. Very strong.

FEET. Forefeet, larger than hind, may be slightly turned out. Pads should be thick and strong. Thin and ferrety feet are objectionable.

He has to dig his way into cairns and dens, and his footing must always be good, hence the importance of the feet.

TAIL. Short, well furnished with hair, but not feathery; carried gaily, but should not turn down towards back.

Self-explanatory, but one word of warning, a tail can be too short, as well as too long, and thus spoil the whole symmetry of the little fellow.

COAT. Very important. Must be double-coated, with profuse, hard, but not coarse, outer coat, and undercoat which resembles fur, and is short, soft and close. Open coats are objectionable. Head should be well furnished.

The importance of this item cannot be over-stressed for the health and comfort of the dog. The harsh outer coat acts as an umbrella and keeps the rain off, and when working in water, one good shake and the bulk of the moisture is off, while the undercoat helps to keep him warm. The coat should not be as hard as a door-mat, as I have seen in some advertisements, however. The coat can be both too short or too long, and the head can be plain, explaining the reiteration of good furnishings being essential.

COLOUR. Red, sandy, grey, brindled, or nearly black. Dark points such as ears and muzzle, very typical.

In short, any colour between black and white. It is clear that the various colours confuse some people and make them think that there are many types of Cairns, while there are breeders who state that no colour, but the colour they happen to be showing, is right. My own view is that from the point of view of money-making, it would have paid better to have one colour. Nothing looks smarter than a bright red dog with a dark face, ears and point to his tail—it is a seller. On the other hand, the Cairn was brought to his present position through many colours, and a litter may have all these if big enough. A good Cairn can't be a bad colour, and colour does not affect disposition, I am delighted to say.

WEIGHT AND SIZE. Ideal weight 14 lb.

Hereby hangs a tale, and it was only in 1922 that this compromise was arrived at, and like all compromises, if not carefully studied, leads to disaster. Prior to this there were two weights, one for the dog and a lighter one for the bitch. Originally there were no weights, but in 1916, the dog was 12 to 16 lb, and the bitch 11 to 14. Why the lady should have the same work to do and be lighter was always difficult to understand, and as the dog was intended to be kept as a worker, the compromise was arrived at. It was agreed that 16 lb was on the heavy side and 11 lb on the light side. However, size must also be taken into account under this heading. A dog can be 'shelly' giving him size but not weight, and 'tubby' without giving him size. So when sizing up the dog, great care must be exercised to strike the happy medium of size to give him agility, yet with enough substance to enable him to hold his own when in a fight that is life and death.

FAULTS. Muzzle; undershot or overshot. Eyes; too prominent or too light. Ears; too large or round at points; they must not be heavily coated with hair. Coat; silkiness or curliness objectionable; a slight wave permissible. Nose; flesh or light coloured most objectionable. In order to keep this breed to the best old working type, any resemblance to a Scottish Terrier will be considered objectionable.

These faults accentuate where the points already set out can go wrong, and show the difficulty the original protagonists of the breed had in keeping the dog away from the standards of their relatives, the Skyes, Scotties, and Westies, and the now defunct Roseneath, Clydesdale and Paisley. Well furnished head, but not as much as the Skye; medium leg but not as short as the Scottie, strong head but not like his long foreface; not so heavy as the Westie and slimmer built; the founders of the club knew what they wanted and also what they did not want.

SCALE OF POINTS

Skull	5
Muzzle	10
Eyes	5
Ears	5
Body	20
Shoulders, Legs and Feet	20
Tail	5
General Appearance (Size and Coat)	30
	100

This hundred would mean perfection which has never yet been attained.

What should come in to the show ring that will attract the judge at once? A shaggy dog with a wedge-shaped head, small sharp-pointed ears without hairy edges, big strong teeth when examined, a friendly 'mischievous' eye, and black nose, on a lithe neck, medium coat and tail to balance his medium level back, no dip, elbows below his body, and straight legs from sloping shoulders attached to a good chest, driven forward by powerful hindquarters, walking on a loose lead as if, not only the show, but the whole earth belonged to him. So your dog starts with almost 70 points before the details are gone into. This standard would be of little use without a little more; and the table on p. 17 therefore must also be studied.

CHAPTER TWO

GREAT DOGS OF THE PAST AND PRESENT

THE CAIRN WAS first registered and exhibited in variety classes as short-haired or prick-eared Skye Terriers. The first time they had a class of their own was at Inverness in 1909, and the judge was the wellknown authority on canine matters, Mr Theo Marples, F.Z.S., Lancashire. His remarks on the dogs then shown are interesting as he looked on them as working terriers and judged them as such. He considered that they were nearer the West Highland White Terrier—then coming into vogue—than the Skye Terrier, and forecast a great future for them. This proved to be true though it was not to reach its zenith for some forty years.

Other shows gave classes and the question of nomenclature was brought to a head when Sir Claud Alexander, the leading Skye Terrier upholder, headed a deputation to the Kennel Club in April 1910, to object to the use of the name Skye Terrier in any shape or form. After full consideration, the Kennel Club granted the name Cairn Terrier, and this was registered under British, Colonial, and Foreign dogs until May 1912, when the breed was granted a separate register.

The best way to establish a breed is to form a club with members who are not only enthusiastic but carry weight and experience, and this was done in 1910, in Edinburgh. Then the need for a standard of points was decided on and a standard drawn up, so that everyone could have some idea of what to expect when they went to look for a Cairn Terrier. This Club was called the Cairn Terrier Club and their rules laid down two important points as the reason for its existence. First to promote the breeding of the old Working Terrier of the Highlands, now known as the Cairn Terrier, and secondly to adopt and publish a description of type and standard as herein stated.

In working out the pedigrees of the earlier dogs it is quite evident that while there was a great deal of 'pedigree unknown' and 'unregistered' there was also a lot of Scottish Terrier and West Highland White blood used. As the three are one stock in origin, they blended fairly well but white pups were not uncommon and the longer head took some time to breed out. After 1924, the use of white blood was banned by the Kennel Club, and could not be legitimately used, and the breed for the future was on its own, to its great benefit.

The Kennel Club granted challenge Certificates for four shows in 1912, and the first was at Richmond, the judge being Mrs Alastair Campbell, the first secretary of the Club. She awarded the certificates to Firring Fling and Firring Flora, both belonging to Messrs Ross and Markland. Both dogs were Highland bred, but one at the show was Loch Scolter out of the West and this affix and the prefix of 'Firring' can be found in most of the pedigrees of today. At Doncaster these decisions were upset, and the judge put the dog second and the bitch third, with Skye Crofter getting the dog certificate. At Edinburgh, this dog got his second certificate, and Tibbie of Harris her first. The Crystal Palace brought in the Hon. Mary Hawke as judge and she confirmed Tibbie, and put up a new dog, Gesto, whose sire was a White Westie. So the first fateful year ended with Crofter and Tibbie having won two certificates each. 1913 came in with 11 shows offering certificates, showing how quickly the breed had established itself. Who was to own the first Champion in the breed, was the absorbing question.

The honour fell to Lady Sophie Scott of Harris, with her home-bred Ch Tibbie of Harris, which is as it should be—ladies first on two or four legs. This show was at Birmingham.

The first Dog Champion got his qualifying certificate at Ayr and became Ch Gesto, bred by Mr Mackinnon in Skye. At the end of the year we had these two and also Ch Firring Frolic and Ch Skye Crofter, with Ch Shiela of Harris—three dogs and two bitches. Of the owners and breeders of these beginnings of the breed, none remain with us, but their memory will always be green while Cairns exist. In 1914, only three champions qualified, in 1915, four, and in 1916, two, when the war got too serious for showing and the Kennel Club cut out shows.

Ch Oudenarde Magic Sired by Ch Oudenarde Midnight Chimes

This might be called the first era of the Cairn, for after the war the change in circumstances began to make itself felt as the old Highland families were going out, the shooting tenants were dropping off, the Americans were becoming interested in our breed, and new breeders were coming in. One of the tragedies to the breed was that during the war, after the shows stopped, Lady Burton, who had been building up her 'Dochfours' had a kennel fire and lost practically all her dogs, and had to start again from scratch. Her first Champion was Dochfour Kyle in 1924, a hard-bitten, racy cairn.

Having seen the first classes for Cairns judged at Inverness, I have seen the steady improvement in showing and handling, and some dogs and owners stick in the memory. Maclennan of the

'Carngowans' had reds chiefly, and his 'Ailsaveg' was a lovely bitch and with the genuine expression; Lady Burton of the Dochfours, with 'Dochfour Vennach', as fine a grey as I have ever handled; Mrs Forbes, with her 'Ross-shire Warrior', a great-bodied dog with character; Mrs Fleming, with her 'Fisherman out of the West', a wonderful red and as good a showman as his mistress was; Mrs Basset with 'Ian of Frimley', a brindle gentleman; the great 'Gille of Hyver' with his devoted Mrs Stephen; Aljck Mackenzie with his 'Moccasin Linda'; Willie Moyes with 'Bogton Brindie'; Miss Irving with 'Beechacre Blaeberry'; Major Townley and 'Fifinella of Carysfort'; and Mrs Dixon with her 'Divor of Gunthorpe', carry us into the thirties where we find Mrs Prichard with her 'Donnington Cheeky' and Miss Reoch with her 'Valiant Pirate'. All these were champions and remained in the country to strengthen the breed for many years. It would be wearisome to recount all those I handled in the ring but the war in 1939 left about two dozen dogs and bitches with one or two certificates and by the time peace came they had little or no chance of completing their title.

On the 15th of January, 1933, there was whelped a dog that was to have a very big influence on the breed at the present day. He was a great dog in himself, and his influence as a sire is clear at every show. This was Ch Splinters of Twobees owned by Miss Bengough and Mrs Butterworth, and he won some eight certificates under the leading judges. But he was shown too often in poor condition as his owners wished him to be seen at his best and his worst. He was a red originally but got darker as he grew older, but his stock were chiefly light coloured with few dark ones. He handed on his good points and when they missed a generation, they came back in the next. The leading dogs of the present day practically all have Splinters' blood to a more or less degree, and carry his sweet disposition. I admired him when I first saw him at Crufts shown with his coat ragged, and discussed him with his owner. It was decided to have him stripped and to show him in three months. It was thought he would be champion in another three, and he was.

As soon as peace was restored, more or less, the breed clubs ap-

plied for championship shows and the three clubs were granted
this and got going. It should be borne in mind, however, that they
could start quicker than the big all-breed shows. The Cairn Terrier Club held the first championship show in Scotland on 29th
May 1946 in Edinburgh with Lady Burton judging, and the first
post-war certificates were won by Valiant Rob Roy of Rhosbridge, and the bitch Knipton Buntylow got the other. In July the
Southern C.T.C. show, where I was judging, confirmed the dog,
but the bitch was Normanhurst Penelope; The Cairn Terrier Association Show came in September and Major Townley confirmed the last show; while at the C.T.C. second show in
November, my friend the late Archie Cameron confirmed Lady
Burton's placings. So ended the year 1946 and it is worthy of note
that Penelope won three other certificates before being exported
to France, while Buntylow won no more. Rob Roy won five
others before being retired to stud, and passed away at a ripe old
age in his own home at Broughty Ferry, Dundee.

By the year 1951, there was an even rhythm in the shows, and it
was easier to see the steady progress of the breed. Champions were
increasing and the rate from then was roughly 11 of both sexes per
annum, with the bitches having 43 as against the dogs 34 down to
1957. The difference between the sexes was due to two causes—
breeding from the bitches which puts them out for a period, and
one or two dogs getting to the top and staying there. This will be
discussed under Shows and Showing. It is decidedly difficult to
pin-point all the good dogs of that time, but those that linger in my
memory are Ch Fincairn Gillian, a lovely red bitch, the best of a
good litter; Ch Lynwil MacIan Dhu, a hard-bitten grey; Ch Rogie
of Rossarden, a bright red; Ch Redletter McRuffie; Ch Unique
Cottage Black Gold, Ch Oudenarde Souvenir and Ch Merrymeet
Jason.

One of the greatest winning bitches of all time, was one shown
in more recent years by her owner/breeder W. N. Bradshaw. Ch
Redletter Moonracker won twenty certificates at the twenty-
seven Championship Shows in which she competed. In 1972 she
won the Group at L.K.A. and went on to be Best Bitch in Show.
Unfortunately, this beautiful bitch died young, without ever

having a litter, although the line is still available through her brother Ch Redletter Moonstruck. The dam of these Champions was herself a great winning bitch Ch Redletter Marcel, having eighteen certificates, thirteen Best of Breed and nine reserve certificates to her credit. She won the Terrier Group at Darlington in 1970. Mr Bradshaw and the Redletter Kennel have done a great deal for the breed and they are the only Cairn Kennel to have twice won Best in Show at an all breeds Championship Show.

One of the strongest male lines must be at the Oudenarde Kennel, owned by Mrs Hamilton and Miss H. Hamilton, Ch Oudenarde Sandboy was the sire of Ch Oudenarde Midnight Chimes. Midnight Chimes sired Ch Oudenarde Midnight Marauder who sired Ch Oudenarde Sea Hawk and Ch Oudenarde Raiding Light. Raiding Light sired Ch Oudenarde Bold and Free and Ch Oudenarde Fair Nicola. Sea Hawk, Bold & Free and Fair Nicola each obtained their titles in 1974. As can be seen from the foregoing, there are now five generations of Champions all from the same line, which must mean that the males in this line not only produce good winning stock, but also pass on the ability to reproduce it in their progeny.

Another kennel which will leave its mark on the breed is the Brucairns, owned by Mrs J. E. Harding. Twice this kennel have won Best of Breed at Crufts, in 1969 with Ch Brucairn Red Robin and again in 1971 with Ch Brucairn Juliet. One judge in the critique described a Brucairn winner as a true Cairn, outgoing and unafraid, obviously brought up in a natural, happy environment. This statement brings the whole picture of the Brucairn Kennel to life, and is indeed a compliment.

It is on these breeders, and others like them, that the future generations of Cairns and Cairn breeders depend, and their future would seem in very good hands.

Ch Brucairn Juliet B.O.B. Crufts 1971

CHAPTER THREE

BUYING A PUP

USUALLY YOUR FIRST introduction to the Cairn is when you see one with a friend; you fall in love with it, and you 'want one the same'. Now forget the last four words as I have never found two Cairns alike in all my experience of them. They are individuals so far as character is concerned, though alike externally. Therefore the wise thing is to ask your friend where it came from and how it was bred, and you should not be very far out. If possible, visit the kennels and see them and any dogs that are for sale. Then pay the price you can afford, but don't try to beat the breeder down. If you can't afford it, then you will have to go elsewhere. Before this you will have learned whether your friend's Cairn is a dog or bitch and if you take my advice and want the best companion, take the lady. I remember once four bitch puppies arriving for me in a box, and they were much admired by the young clerkesses. One of them said how much she would love one of them and I said 'then have one as a gift'. But the moment she knew it was a bitch she did not want it, and the reason given was that 'all the dogs in the country would be after it from time to time'. She seemed to forget that one of these dogs might be hers and she would be sitting up all night waiting for him, swearing he would get a thrashing when he came home, and then when he did at 2 a.m., she would be so glad to see him that he was hugged and not thrashed. Bitches are more affectionate, easier trained, don't require to be walked a mile before going to bed—the 'Lamp-post' joke is a stern reality—and when in season have merely to be locked up and the key in your pocket, and then exercised at night. Carry her for about 200 yards from the house and then set her down, but on the lead, of course, and all interested dogs start there and stop there, and you have no trouble at your front door. That is my own personal view; however, there is something about a dog that is different and he is more independent, but it is for you to decide.

If you have the choice of picking one, take the brightest and liveliest, keep to a dark eye, but please yourself for colour as it does not count in the ring—if you get there. Look at the hind legs for dew-claws, rudimentary toes that should be removed within a day or two of birth, for if the puppies are about three months, they may then have to be removed by a Vet. Normally the breeder will have done this at the right time. Avoid any signs of shyness, as it is very difficult to get rid of. See that the tail is matching the body for length, and that the ears are small and pointed. If not erect then ask the seller about this, as if they are tipped over and big, there is a risk of them not coming up. This, I am glad to say, is decidedly rare now, but it does happen. The pup should always be plump up to 3 months, like a baby. If not there may be something wrong, such as worms.

If the pup is to be reared as a companion, and a companion only, then the younger you get him the better but not earlier than 6 weeks, preferably at 8 weeks. Training a pup does not start then, but educating him does, and you will be surprised to find how early he begins to size things up. This, of course, means that you have plenty of time at your disposal, but after all the friendship is to last for some ten to 15 years or more and it is worth the early start. Three months should be the oldest to buy, in my view, where companionship is the sole or main object of the purchase. Remember also that he is to be a watch, and so far as his size enables him, a guard.

You are often told to go to a big kennel, and there is nothing wrong with this advice but never forget that the small kennel may be in a position to give more individual attention to its dogs and that means a lot. Both can be quite reliable, and both may be the reverse. Be sure that you have got all details before you take the little fellow away, find out how he has been fed, and if any attempt at cleanliness has been made, get his exact age and the pedigree, and then take him home. He may cry a little at first but this soon passes in a well-fed, and comfortably-housed pup.

It may be, of course, that you are unable to visit any kennels and then you are in a difficult position as I would never recommend buying puppies of that age on approval. I recommend, therefore, that you get in touch with some one who knows the secretary or president or some of the officials of the club which fosters the breed, and you will find yourself in touch with people who know the dog, and will see that you get value for money. It is not in their interests to have a newcomer disappointed. If you can't do this, then write to the Kennel Club and you will find a courteous body who will put you in touch with the clubs.

Very often after purchase, a pup changes his outlook, and it rests with the new owner to tide him over this period. Have you ever been homesick? I have. The pup comes away from company, brothers and sisters, and dam, and hears only a strange voice, however kind, and food that is a little different. How would you like to be put in a box for many hours in a noisy train, and then find yourself in China, where not a word of the language means anything to you. That is what happens when a puppy comes from the Islands, where only Gaelic is spoken. Even an adult dog has to learn English.

Therefore, if you are to get the best out of your pal for the 10 or 15 years or more that you are to be together, you want patience and understanding, a kind voice and a kinder hand, and you will reap a rich reward in love and affection.

If the puppy arrives by train, open the box in a closed room or shed so that there is no possibility of his escaping and bear in mind that he may want to relieve himself. Some newspapers spread on the floor will prove more than useful. Talk to him and make a fuss of him, and let him have a dish of water as he will probably be thirsty; but do not feed him for an hour or so, otherwise he may stuff himself and vomit. I recommend warm milk with some bread or biscuit soaked in it for the start.

If you take the puppy by car, put him in a box, even a cardboard one, as if there is a longish journey and he gets into a draught, he can easily get a chill. I had a friend whose dog was regularly getting a chill, and after carefully checking up, it was found that he lay on the floor of the car where an unnoticed draught came in. When he was made to sit on a seat, there were no more troubles. He was an adult dog, too. In the next chapter we will consider the question of training him to be house-clean and not a nuisance, to himself and others.

3 month old puppy before ears are erect, and still with 'puppy fluff'

CHAPTER FOUR

FEEDING AND CARE OF A PUPPY

IT IS DIFFICULT to say what is most important in the handling of a puppy as no two are alike, but in my view feeding wants careful thought, and no two people think alike. In Scotland, and particularly in the North, porridge made of oatmeal, with milk, has always been looked on as a staple article of diet, though I saw this condemned in an article the other day. In shepherds' agreements in the old days there was always a clause as to the amount of meal he was to be allowed for his dogs, and if the dogs were able to do the heavy work called for on a hill sheep-farm on this diet, then it cannot be without value. At six weeks there should be six meals a day and at three months this reduced to about four, keeping in view that it is a question of little and often. A little minced raw meat should be given daily, but apart from the normal meals, so that it is looked on as an extra or dainty by the puppy, and you will be surprised how quickly he starts to 'size things up'. Preferably the meat should be scraped and lean in any case. A small teaspoonful will be enough to begin with increasing with age. Some dogs are not keen on raw meat, but this is their natural and best food, and the sooner they get the taste for it the better. You often see pups with 'pot-bellies', as they are called, and may have seen this at the kennel where you purchased your pup. This is a sign of overfeeding and often wrong feeding, but most probably worms. You cannot go wrong with milk puddings, arrowroot or bread soaked in milk but this should be varied judiciously, and not made too sloppy. A toasted crust, dry and hard will be appreciated and helps the teeth and gums. A big bone, raw or cooked, with gristle adhering, is appreciated and also helps teeth and gums. I have avoided a lecture on vitamins, as I feel a Veterinary Surgeon is more qualified to write on this aspect than a simple dog breeder.

I have always made it a rule that the puppy has a box of his own—Sanctuary in a Deer Forest—where no one can touch him

r punish him by word or hand. When in trouble he makes for it
nd you always know where to get him. He keeps his bones and
oys there, a pair of the master's old slippers, a ball, all valuable to
im, and he quickly knows this.

A puppy can't help wetting often and it does not strike him as
vrong until you explain this to him. Beating him and rubbing his
ose in it, no doubt will effect a cure, but I don't recommend this.
Get your catch phrase—mine being 'Who did it?'—and when he
apses, use it. Tell him good dogs don't do this and talk to him. He
as brains and will appreciate it. Always put him out the first
hing in the morning and the last thing at night; after every meal;
nd if you see him wake up out of a sound sleep. It all takes time,
ut it is worth it and does not last long.

I know that at the beginning of the last war when children by the
housands were evacuated from towns to country, I had my eyes
opened, as I had something to do with it. The number of grown
children who were 'bed-wetters' and came to homes that had
never met with this, caused untold trouble and friction, and some
care and training at the beginning would have cut out a lot of it. In
a matter of weeks the trouble will cease in most cases, and when
you take the puppy out, if you have the time, see him clean himself
and tell him what a clever little chap he is and see his tail wag as he
realizes that he has given you pleasure—his whole object in life
and the years to come.

I do realize that some puppies can be very trying and some take
a long time to reach a reasonable standard, but never lose your
temper or the training goes back weeks or months. Get him used
to being handled and picked up, not by the scruff of the neck, but
with both hands under him. He will use his teeth and maybe
scratch, but that is his way of showing affection, and with his
tongue. If he goes too far, have your catch word ready, 'Naughty',
or 'not good', or simply 'no', and it is soon understood.

As he gets on, the food can be drier and you can make a standard of any of the popular brands of biscuit—fed dry or soaked—
but he is a house-dog and will expect little extras and the much
maligned 'scraps' from the table. I never believe in a pup going on
the lead before six months but a collar can go on at three months,

which may take the form of stout string or anything like that.

Usually his box will be in the kitchen and for some time the floor should be covered with newspapers, and if a mistake is made it is easily put right. I found in one case that by taking out a spoiled paper and putting the puppy on it, he understood, and there was always an old paper outside, to which he went. Puppies should have as much freedom as possible and grass to run on, but if you take him out for a walk, always remember that he has to come back and so make the distance suit this fact. Overdoing walking on the road at this age can affect his legs and feet.

In America, there has been a series of experiments on this feeding question which is very interesting and you can consider it. The theory put forward is that a dog (originally a wild animal) gorges food as he is afraid that he may not get any more for a long time. So if there is always a 'balanced' diet available for him, in less than no time, he just goes and eats when he wants it. The photos of the dogs certainly showed them in good condition. Some years ago I sold a dog to a friend who believed in this idea, without knowing anything about the above experiments, and there always was a dish with food placed in the house where the dog could get to it, as well as water. It was replenished from time to time and varied, and the dog is now $10\frac{1}{2}$ years and as fit as the proverbial fiddle.

I leave you to make your choice as I am never dogmatic when there are proved alternatives.

To vary the diet, fish is very good, but be careful of bones; tripe cooked and uncooked is good, and relished; liver is excellent and the 'lights', in small quantities, helps the stomach; the throat (or thrapple as it was called when I was a boy) is good cooked or raw and helps like bones. For a puppy, only small quantities are needed, and your butcher usually will be helpful when he knows it is for a puppy.

At this stage it is as well to consider distemper although it will be dealt with in a later chapter. Unfortunately I am an anti-vaccinationist to the extent that I don't believe in vaccination as a preventative for Smallpox, and would not have it done. On the other hand, if I had to have it done to go to Canada, there is no

way out, and it is done. So with inoculation of puppies for distemper, I won't have it done but that does not mean that I tell you
not to have it done. Discuss the matter with your Vet, who would
be called in for any trouble, and take his advice. I have heard and
seen both sides of the question and new vaccines come out from
time to time so I advertise none, but always 'take your Vet's
advice'.

CHAPTER FIVE

TRAINING

THE FIRST THING you want to make up your mind on is what you are to train your dog for. If it is to take him to the Obedience Shows and make him an exhibit, and winner there, that is one thing; but if it is to have an obedient pal and friend, and one who will guard you to the extent of warning you of danger, that is quite a different matter. In America the Cairn Terrier is well known at the Obedience Tests and gets full marks as often as not, but he has not been put into this contest much in this country—for which am personally very thankful. I consider that it takes away from his spirit and *joie de vivre*, which is his greatest attraction. The routine for a gun-dog is that he sits, lies down, fetches and carries and in short it is wonderful to see how well he works up to the game—but this takes a lot of training and is a professional's job, and is not suitable for a Cairn.

First, we get him used to a collar and then the lead goes on, and he kicks at this naturally, but a little patience and a pat or two and he gets to know that it is nothing to be afraid of. I always keep the leads and collars hanging where the dogs can see them and they know, when they come down, that there is a walk in store and so they love their leads. Time and patience are of the essence. He will pull at first, or sulk behind, but a gentle tug soon gets him moving onwards. The desire to pull means a sharp jerk back and a word (say 'Steady now') and inside two or three lessons, you have him well started, for he is a small dog and easily controlled.

I admit that some dogs never quite respond and this also applies to show dogs. All dogs should walk on a loose lead, but many won't. He should walk at your side thus.

If you wish to train him to sit (he can be taught in the house) tell him to do so and press him into that position. Lying down is the same. The more you talk to him, the easier it becomes to get him to understand, and while I do not say that a dog understands every

34

word you say, he does understand the tones and inflexions of your voice better than a human being does.

If you own a car, he should be encouraged to jump into it when told to or asked. Cairns love cars. Once in, they must be trained not to jump out until told to. This is very essential as otherwise he might jump into traffic. When I stop the car, I always say 'No, stay there' which he does. When he is wanted to go out 'Walkie' is my word. When his walk is over or I want him on the lead sooner—'Collar on'—brings him back at once, but I soon found that the car was the rallying point, and that was not to be lost sight of. In other words I take full advantage of the little fellow's intelligence, and he quickly trains himself.

Of course, most owners have other things to do than train their dog, and training has to be fitted into their spare time, which is quite a simple matter and also a great pleasure. Don't make any lesson too long.

There is another point, (and it is very much like the joke about the small boy who always dodges having his face washed) and that is to get him used to the comb and brush. The brush can start at three months, and the pup will not like it at first, but a few kindly words, and only a little to start with, and gradually he will look forward to it. Personally I prefer a wire comb like Spratt's No. 6 (and don't believe that other sizes are just as good) or similar in all respects. It clears out all dead coat, and especially dead undercoat, and if there happens to be an odd flea, it comes out also. Brush if you like but you don't want to polish the Cairn or put a gloss on him as he is a rugged little fellow.

I don't believe in washing unless it is absolutely necessary, and some dogs will roll themselves in filth whenever they see it and even go out of their way to find it. I have never been able to understand why. Then you *must* wash, and I use ordinary carbolic soap, which is always on hand for personal use. The first wash is the worst, as it is new and strange to the dog. I use a deep tub with soapy water and lift him into it and stand him there, and then lather from the tail upwards, doing the head last and making sure that no suds go into his eyes or ears. Then still standing in the tub, he is rinsed out with lukewarm water, as much as possible squeezed out of his coat, and then thoroughly dried with a rough towel. If possible do this in warm weather and then give him a run in grass to shake himself and roll, and all is well.

There are two debatable points which we might consider here. Is he to be allowed to occupy the easiest chair in the house? If not then start early and discourage him from chair or sofa jumping—it may be difficult I can assure you.

If he is to travel in the car, he may be car sick, and some dogs never get over it. In that case you must carry newspapers or old dusters to clean up, as this is not a thing that can be avoided by training. However I have heard of a cure and know of it being successful with dogs in two cases, and children in one, but why it should be so I do not know. Take a piece of chain or soft wire and attach it to the chassis in the rear so that it touches the road as the car runs. No doubt many of you have seen this and wondered as I did. I enquired and checked; without the chain, sickness occurred, with it, it did not. In the three cases mentioned, it definitely worked and as it costs nothing to try, you can do so. If it does not work, you can drop it.

Next you have the nails to attend to, although not so much as in a show dog. Some breeders begin cutting the nails at six weeks and do it weekly, as near to the quick as possible without drawing blood. The idea is that this makes the dog stand better on his feet. In addition the little sharp nails fix in woollens, carpets, etc. Personally I examine the nails about once a month, and if curled over the toes, clip them. On the other hand if the dog is regularly exercised, especially on the road, the nails take care of themselves for a companion dog. At the same time, the Cairn is a demon for digging if he gets half a chance, and this keeps his nails in order—though this is a doubtful blessing in a garden.

Firmness is necessary, and if an order is given, it must be obeyed, and you should never give it unless you have time to see it carried out. Otherwise the dog can become indifferent. See it from the dog's point of view if possible.

I sold a dog to a friend and it was a great pal and a success, but one day I received a letter saying that they were considering eturning it for disobedience. However, a visitor had advised them o write to me first. My friends lived in the country about 20 miles)ut and the little fellow was expected to go into town by car when vanted. When the car arrived at the front door, he refused to go in and the result was that first his master went after him, followed by his mistress, and only after he had the entire household running after him, would he jump into the car. One day the train for London was missed, at which point I received my letter. The solution was simple. The car was put in front of the house—when no one was going anywhere—and the circus started, but this time when he went in, he was shown the whip and got two light cuts (as much as his owner could stand). It never happened again. But see t from the dog's point of view. It was a wonderful game and he enjoyed it and no doubt he was annoyed when he found that his master and mistress did not appreciate it. Moral: never run after the dog, make him come to you, and pick the time when you can make him understand this. Once understood he will carry on, but remember that he must come to you as he loves you and not as he fears you, or some day he will fear too much, and not come.

CHAPTER SIX

SHOWING AND WHAT IT MEANS

ANY A PURCHASER of a companion has become a winner at shows often merely through a friend suggesting that the little fellow can win. It is nice to be able to say that your dog has won some prizes. There is also the other side, and that is if you are happy with your dog you should try to support the shows in some way. If in the course of time, at the ripe age of ten to fifteen years, your pal goes to the happy hunting grounds, you will find that you wish to replace him, and with the same blood if possible.

You will not be able to do this if there are no shows, for exhibitors and breeders are kept in existence by these competitions. It is therefore to be hoped that you will in no matter how small a way give them some support.

Often I receive letters—many of them tear-stained—asking me where a dog of the same breeding as the one that has died can be bought. 'Knowing the ropes' as they say, I can usually help with the necessary information. It will be of interest therefore to know a little of how the machine works.

No doubt when dog showing started it was a sport, and in those leisured days the shows went on for days, the *cognoscenti* discussing the breeds and their good and bad points, buying and selling, and generally making it a holiday. Others called it a game, and at times it still is this, and in the worst sense of the word. Others make it a business, and you can usually get good treatment here, as they are proud of their reputation in and out of the show ring.

Anyhow you wish to show, but before you do so, make up your mind that if you lose, you are not to break your heart—you still have a little fellow devoted to you in weal or woe, and you must return the compliment in success or defeat.

The ruling body of the dog world is the Kennel Club, 1/4 Clarges Street, Piccadilly, London, and this body grew up like Topsy. Don't let people talk to you about the English Kennel

Club; it is not that. It is *The* Kennel Club and came first and still is looked to as the world wide guiding authority in dog matters. Something we in Britain should be proud of. Always remember that if things go wrong, or you make mistakes, the above is the address to write to for guidance and help, and you will be sure to get it.

I recommend any novice to begin at the bottom and not to launch out into the fierce competition of a championship show straight away, on the ground of expense and inexperience.

EXEMPTION CLASSES. These are usually held at agricultural shows, fêtes for charity, etc., and only four pedigree classes are allowed by the Kennel Club. Your dog does not need to be registered and entry is on the ground. I have seen an absolute novice going to one of these entertainments with her dog on a lead, being cajoled into showing it, and, having taken two first prizes, she was struck with the disease of showing and has been at it ever since. This is a cheap way of starting, and these shows are very useful on the social side in making friends and getting to know the rudiments of the sport. Often there are tacked on half a dozen or more 'novelty' classes for the fattest, the leanest, the longest-tailed, etc., dogs, and these are judged by different judges from the other four classes and are good 'ice-breakers' and friendship-formers. Of course you can get some good dogs here where 'pot-hunting' is not unknown. Do not forget, however, that the show is held under Kennel Club Rules and permission.

SANCTION SHOWS. These are confined to the members of a club, or society holding the show, and this means that you must join the club, which is easily done by getting in touch with the secretary. It is usually held on Saturday afternoon or the local half holiday, and often in the evening after 5 p.m. There is no benching and it is very informal. There may be only one breed shown, but more usual, every breed is shown in what are called 'variety' classes, just as in the Exemption classes. If possible always enter your dog in the breed class so that he meets his own kind and you can thus form a relative opinion as to whether he can go into stronger competition. In variety classes you may find a Chihuahua competing against a St Bernard, but this gives no guide as to their position in their own breed. All dogs must be registered here, but it gives both dog and exhibitor cheaper experience than the higher-up shows and the venue is usually at your own door. Champions are barred owing to there being no Open classes, etc.

LIMITED SHOWS. All these have some qualifying clause or restriction as to number of classes, area in which the exhibitor must reside, or that it includes membership to some club, breed or otherwise. This is always very clearly set out and mistakes should not be made, unless through great carelessness. They are just a stiffer Members' or Sanction show, where greater competition may be expected.

OPEN SHOWS. At this show, any dog can compete, either in his own breed or in the variety classes. It should be kept in mind that the show committee try to make the show a success, especially on the financial side. If a class is given for a breed, the prize money is usually £1.75p in three prizes, and as the entry money is usually 50p, unless there are at least 4 dogs entered, there is a loss. If you are keen on your breed, then enter and support, and to help further have an entry in some variety class.

CHAMPIONSHIP SHOWS. There is no difference between this and an Open show except on one point and that is that Challenge Certificates are offered, and these are awarded to the best dog and best bitch in each breed. Any show committee that wishes to be given 'Championship Status' applies to the Kennel Club, who consider the application and may or may not grant it, and this is applied to the following year. It is not only an honour but a very serious responsibility as the prize money is double that of an Open show, and the Kennel Club see to it that the guarantors will be able to carry out their obligations. At present there are 28 Championship shows giving classes for our breed.

The biggest Championship show in the world is Crufts, now run by the Kennel Club, and a win there is looked on as very special indeed. For your dog to become a champion, three certificates have to be won under three different judges, and this is a simple and easily understood system compared with the countries run on the points system, where you are never quite sure of the results until the ruling body do the counting up. The win may vary in value from 1 to 4 or 5 points, or even nothing. As a further guide, it should be understood that there are usually three prizes and a reserve, the latter merely meaning that in the event of a disqualification of any dog in front, each dog moves up one step, and the reserve gets at least the third prize. The reserve to the Certificate winner however does not move up automatically, but has to be certified by the judge as worthy to move up.

A British Champion has a very high standing in most of the countries of the world.

K.C. GAZETTE. This is really for the Club secretaries and the exhibiting world, but still is interesting to the dog lover. It contains the minutes of meetings of the K.C. Committee, applicants for prefixes, all dogs registered or exchanged, exports, notes on leading shows, etc. It is issued monthly and the whole idea is to keep those interested in touch with the dog world. There may be wrong registrations, or applications for prefixes, etc., and you can help by pointing this out, although the ruling powers are very careful. At the same time you see the reports on any persons who have broken the rules, and this may save you a lot of trouble when you are buying—*cave canem*. If you register your dog, you will find him here.

K.C. STUD BOOK. This is a gold mine of information, giving you the names of the certificate winners for the year, the addresses of the owners, list of prefixes, all Clubs and Societies with the secretaries' addresses, etc. In short no secretary can afford to be without it (and I hope that some of my readers will take an interest in secretarial work some day, as though very trying at times, it is always interesting, and essential if the dogs are to be kept in existence).

REGISTRATION. Your dog should always be registered whether the idea is to show him or not. Your motto should be 'Do it now'. When you purchase your puppy you should insist on getting form 1A, for registration of one dog, completed and handed over. If it has already been registered, then get the transfer form signed and completed instead. It should then be registered with the Kennel Club and the necessary fee paid. Should you decide to breed or give a service to a friend, then there is no trouble on the question of pedigree. If either or both of the parents are not registered already, you have an extra fee to pay, and over and above that, you may have a lot of trouble in getting any registration as the Kennel Club are becoming more and more strict on the question of purity of breed, and rightly so. In any case of doubt, tell the correct facts to the Kennel Club and they will always help you out, but don't try bluff or terminological inexactitudes, as they probably know far more about that than you do.

In addition to prizes and certificates, there is another card that some breeders are very keen on and that is the Junior Warrant. A dog is a Junior until he is 18 months old, and you can only show him when he is 6 months old at least. Accordingly you have one year in which to win this, and you require 25 points to do so. For every win at an Open show you get 1 point and at a Championship 3 points, in breed classes only where Challenge Certificates are on offer, otherwise it is only 1 point, so that if you have a 'good day' at a Championship show, you can amass quite a number.

There is another certificate you can get if you breed puppies from your bitch, and to my mind the breeding side is the most fascinating. If you breed a good litter there is always a market for it, and should the owner of the stud dog you used hear of it, it does not take him long to get there to see them. You are the breeder, and should the pup become a Champion you get a Certificate from the Kennel Club which is a very great honour, and much less expensive to obtain than to hunt for the three certificates for a champion, maybe for years. I noted the other day that one Cairn took three years, and a dog at that.

If you do breed, don't think that any dog will do, but try to work out what is likely to suit and to give you a better pup than either parent if possible. I refer to this later.

REGISTERED PREFIX. As you can understand, with thousands of names of dogs being registered every year for almost a hundred years now, there can be overlapping and mistakes. To obviate this, the prefix was brought in, very much like your own surname. The simplicity of it is obvious as once you have it, the simplest of names for your dog can be used and very little chance of it not being accepted by the K.C. Try to register 'Pat' and you are certain to have your form returned, but with the prefix 'Clattering' already yours, you are sure to get 'Clattering Pat' without any trouble and no confusion. Essential for a kennel nowadays, and might I ask you to make it short, and avoid copying others when you make your application to the Kennel Club. Many people have used their names backwards—Edwards becoming Sdrawde—Munro becoming d'Ornum, and this is merely a hint for expedition in granting the said prefix.

BREEDING TERMS. This is one of the thorny problems of dogdom and anyone getting or giving a bitch on breeding terms should be very careful to see that both parties understand accurately what it means. There has been a lot of litigation about it, and the Kennel Club are now prepared to register any written agreement between parties for a fee, but it must be clearly understood that they do not make out the agreement or dictate its terms.

There are two forms of the bargain—where the bitch is loaned and therefore the property does not pass, and the bitch returns to the owner after the litter, and secondly where the bitch is given on breeding terms and the property passes.

I have seen many agreements, fair and unfair, but immediate points to be clearly set out are: does the bitch pass from the owner, and if so when; what is to happen to the first litter; if not in whelp when handed over, who pays for the stud service; what of future litters; in the event of there being no puppies, what of the future, who pays for the second service. Many owners give a second service free, but this is not compulsory, but a friendly action. There are other possibilities, and it is better to think them out in advance rather than fall foul of the Kennel Club and find yourself in expensive legislation. In the old days, bargains were chiefly verbal—I will give you the bitch and get half the litter, me having first pick, you second and so on—and it worked smoothly in most cases. In this instance the bitch would be already in whelp, and both sides having a good idea of what happened at the last whelping, hope for equal luck in this one.

SHOWING. Competition is keener now than ever and a few hints may be helpful, especially to the beginner.

The Secretary of a show issues a schedule setting out the rules of the show and also an entry form. If you are to enter you should send the secretary a post card, asking for a schedule, but once you are known as a regular exhibitor, schedules come to you automatically. However, if not received in good time, then send the post card—mistakes do happen. Study the rules carefully, and then read the classes and see which your dog may enter. At the beginning, he is eligible for every class, if under a year old, but the more he wins the less he is eligible for, until finally he is only eligible for Open class.

The completion of the entry form, which is sent to the secretary by a specified date, is simple, and is forwarded along with the necessary cash. The dog's name is inserted, as registered at the Kennel Club, or if the form is with them and not returned to you yet, add the letters N.A.F. (name applied for), or if you have bought the dog registered and the form is with the K.C. for transference then add T.A.F. (transfer applied for). Insert the breed next. State the sex. Next the date of birth. Then the breeder and the sire and dam of the dog. If you are open to sell it, then the price. Lastly the number of each class in which you wish to show the dog, this being taken from the schedule. Then you sign the infectious disease declaration, insert your name and address and for the sake of everyone, read the form over carefully and make sure that there are no mistakes. These cause everyone untold trouble—including yourself—and worst of all, perhaps the loss of a prize

Your first trial is over, as the first entry and show is the most worrying.

PREPARATION FOR SHOW. You are fortunate in the Cairn Terrier in that he requires very little special attention. Dogs cast their coats roughly three times in two years, the first cast being at about 8 months, and a bitch usually comes in season for the first time at this age. Remember, however, that there is no fixed time. Some puppies cast their coats every 6 months, but when they have cast twice you have a fair idea for the future, and in addition you are learning to note the signs.

Take your dog in hand about a month before the show and comb and brush him every two or three days, and thus get all dead coat out. Avoid washing as it softens the coat, but a swim in the sea is an excellent tonic for dog and coat. See that all loose hairs are combed out and that the tail tapers to a point, as it normally does. Get your friends to handle him so that he will be used to strangers and so be at ease when the judge handles him. Every day for half an hour walk him round in a garden or public park clockwise and anti-clockwise with the dog on your right and then on your left, always on the inner side of the circle. This gives the judge the opportunity of seeing your dog at his best.

Later in the day for about the same time, walk him up and down in a straight line, and have a friend if possible to stand and observe this and tell you how the dog looks. Get your friend also to do this and form your own opinion of how he walks. During this time, my strong advice is not to talk to the dog at all, as then he gets into the habit of looking round and putting his ears back for instructions. You win your prizes here by good training and not by bouncing balls and offering titbits to your dog in the ring. Make as much fuss of him as you like before and after his exercise but during it pay strict attention to his walking, and a slight jerk on the lead if he starts slacking.

Do not make these practice periods last longer than half an hour, or he will get bored, and even less to start with. He should also be made to stand firmly on a lead that is not too tight, and from time to time you can halt and do this, as the judge will want all these actions performed. Both of you thus gain confidence in each other, and will repeat this in the ring. I have seen exhibitors in the ring with balls, liver—once a dead rat—all trying to get their dogs to show, instead of doing all this at home. The dog may be nervous at his first show, and especially as a puppy, but this will pass if you have patience. Go into the ring to win and the message passes down the lead to the dog, just as surely as defeatism passes down.

Show him on a slip lead and preferably the one he has been trained on, but you must have a collar that will not slip over his head, and a chain to tie him up in his bench. You can help him a lot for his first show by doing this at home or in the garden, and it will then come as no shock to him at the show. See that the chain is adjusted in such a way that the dog cannot slip off the bench and hang himself, as has happened. Preferably it should have a hook and swivel at each end.

In the old days dogs were watered and fed, but that does not happen now. You must bring a dish for water for him, but as few shows go on after six, I would suggest no food beyond a light snack in the morning and then when he gets home and gets a run in the garden, a meal as usual. Food can make him drowsy and you don't want that during the show. There is no straw, so bring a blanket for him to lie on. Leave your dog, and find out where your ring is, and when the judging starts. Also discover where the secretary's office is, as you may need his help, and where water is to be got for your dog. Remember he must stand first in all things, if you are to get to the top of the tree in the end. You will find other exhibitors beside you and there is no friendlier body than the 'Cairnites' so don't worry.

You are a novice and don't be ashamed of this fact, as they all were at some time or other. The less you know, the more you will learn, and as you have two eyes and two ears but only one tongue, I need say no more. It is clear that you cannot go all day without food, catering may not be good, and there may be queues, not forgetting that you may not want to leave your dog alone too long. So take a light basket with you and put in whatever you think you may require in the way of tea and coffee and sandwiches. My

3 pups approx. 6–9 months old light pup in centre was campaigned to become Ch. Brucairn Merrybelle

Photo. Anne Cumber

remarks about the dog and the meal on getting home, also apply to you. Don't forget your comb for the dog, and a brush if you think it advisable, slip lead, collar and chain, admission ticket, and the removal card that entitles you to take your dog out of the show. A towel is also useful and a small piece of soap.

When you go into the ring have nothing in your hands beyond your comb, to run it over the dog, if necessary after the judge has handled him. Then from the minute you go into the ring have one eye on the judge and the other on dog, and don't fuss and tug him. You trust him and he trusts you. Don't talk to the judge unless he talks to you, and then answer any question courteously and tersely—e.g. Question—What is the age of your dog? Answer—Fifteen months.

I once asked this question and was told the exact date, the sire and dam, and I was afraid I would then be told what he had won. I once told a young exhibitor to have an eye on each, and wished I had stopped there, but I added that a swivel eye would be useful and was met with the reply that she had one. I need not tell you how embarrassed I felt when I found that she had a glass eye, and from that time on I seldom made any remarks.

Win or lose, take it smiling. I want you to be a good winner, which is even more difficult than being a good loser. You wanted the judge's opinion, you paid to get it and you have got it. You think your dog a good one, you may have been told he is a good one, and he may be a good one, but not in this judge's opinion. But only on the day and the day's showing. Of course, he may be a good one, but there were better dogs there again in that judge's opinion. If the judge gives you a hint on any point, make a note of it and benefit. Study the winning dogs with an open mind and see where yours fails, and don't do as many beginners do 'Crib the judge and the winners'. Remember that your thoughts must be on your dog and not on the exhibitors right and left, and be ready to go before the judge at any moment.

Once at Cruft's I was stewarding for a well-known judge. I thought I knew which was the best dog, but I was not the judge. The Challenge Certificate was about to be awarded, when the judge said to me, 'Where is that good red dog?' There was no red dog there, and it was the one I thought would win. I buzzed round the ring and then found the dog with the owner busy in a discussion in a corner about some political matter. I told her the judge wanted to see her dog again, but she said she had no chance of the certificate. The judge called over to me, 'Yes that is the dog I wanted', and five minutes later it had the certificate which could so carelessly have been lost.

Finally if your dog has a temper and is inclined to be pugnacious at times, see that it does not upset other dogs, and try to get to the end of the line. If your dog is inclined to snap at men mention this to the judge courteously.

CHAPTER SEVEN

FIRST AID OR MEDICAL TREATMENT

IT IS A wise thing both with yourself and the dog never to start treatment until you are sure what the disease is. You have only to pick up any newspaper or magazine and you will find enough remedies on sale to cure every disease that was ever known, both for man and beast. Many people believe that a dog must be dosed for worms periodically, whether they have worms or not, largely as a means of so-called prevention.

Dogs do not have colds like human beings and if you see the symptoms of a running nose and 'mattery' eye, you probably have a case of distemper. You should have a medicine cupboard or shelf on which simple remedies are kept for the initial treatment of your dog. These should be used as occasion arises.

One very important one is *Castor Oil*, and where the Cairn shows violent thirst and vomiting, a table-spoonful will work wonders in clearing the irritant out of the stomach. This helps the digestion which has been upset by some foreign matter or a chill.

Epsom Salts is another useful item and it can be given dry by opening the dog's mouth and putting it at the back of the tongue, when it is swallowed. Enough to go on a shilling is a reasonable dose.

If you know your dog has swallowed poison, an emetic, such as washing soda should be given, and the dog taken to the Vet or the Vet taken to the dog, and at once.

Angier's Emulsion is one medicine I always have at hand, as it cannot do harm. Many years ago, I had to use it regularly myself, and as one of my dogs was not too bright or happy in his food and exercise, I thought that as the emulsion did me good, it could hardly harm the dog. I pouched the dog's cheek and poured some in, and when next day the dog looked and behaved better I continued with the treatment. In a week he was all right. Probably he had had a chill on his stomach; my Vet agreed and said that it was always worth a trial. Quite safe to give if diarrhoea is noted.

Benbow's Mixture is a very old and well tried 'tonic' and one which I always have at hand. I have never found a dog that 'likes' it, though some like the above emulsion. It is given for a period of say five to seven days, and then omitted for the same period. It does improve a dog's appetite in my experience. It should not however, be given if there are signs of diarrhoea.

Aspirin is a very old friend and better and safer than many so called tonics and sedatives. For fits or hysteria, you can have no better, as bromide has never struck me as being quick acting. For a Cairn I would say anything from 10 to 15 grains is sufficient and safe, roughly a grain per lb. weight.

Hydrogen peroxide is very useful where there are cuts either caused by another dog, or glass, or thorns. Wash out the wound with a weak solution. If the dog is gashed then consider the Vet. For the head, ears and eyes, it is not the job of any one but a Vet, as untold damage can be done by careless bandaging. Here I refer to amateurs and not to the big kennels, where experienced breeders are handling these things every day, and know exactly how far they can go.

I have twice had dogs with broken legs, and in both cases there was no Vet within 50 miles, and I had the temerity to have a talk with my doctor about it. He assured me that 'healers' would act for anyone in pain, to the best of their ability. Provided I could give the anatomy, he would set the leg in plaster—and he did, and in six weeks the dog was going about looking for more trouble. He gave a dose of 20 grains of aspirin first, as the dog was a strongly built Scottie. My advice is to get the Vet at once or go to him and have the broken bone set and don't 'potter about' with it yourself. I have seen a Saluki break its shoulder blade; the Vet operated on it, wired it up, and the dog won challenge certificates later on, there being not the least sign of a limp.

Skin trouble will happen, and fleas seem to come from nowhere. Your Vet or chemist will tell you of the best flea and lice destroyer, as there are always improvements going on. If the skin is broken, always be careful with D.D.T. preparations. Eczema is more common than mange and more easily dealt with; though when I was a boy, the dog only suffered from two diseases, mange and canker (ear). If mange is suspected, it is best to see your Vet. A very simple and old-fashioned dressing can be got from your chemist and kept handy. Equal parts of paraffin oil and olive oil, and these thickened to the consistency of thick cream with flowers of sulphur, can be rubbed into diseased skin and will keep the dog comfortable, pending developments. Ear Canker, and you know this by the sight and the smell, is a matter for the Vet to guide you, and on no account should advertised cures be poured into the ear.

There are two ways to dose a dog, one for solids and the other for liquids, but the great thing is that the dog must be trained to trust. From puppyhood, a practice should be made of opening the puppy's mouth from time to time, and he gets used to it and knows that there is nothing to fear. As it grows older and stronger in the jaw, the best way is to place the left hand over his upper jaw, the elbow being along the dog's body, the thumb slips into the mouth with the lip over the teeth, and the three fingers on the other side in the same position. The left hand has an immense power in this way, while the right hand holds the pill or non-liquid medicine. The mouth opens as the left fingers press in, and the right finger and thumb can part the jaws and slip the medicine to the back of the tongue, and then touch the front of the tongue, so the dose slips down.

For liquids, the left hand holds the jaws closed, while with the right finger a pouch is made of the right side of the mouth. The head is held up and it is best to have someone to pour the medicine into the pouch, and rub the throat. The liquid oozes through the teeth and the dog swallows quite easily, the left hand being eased a bit for this purpose. This is not so easily explained as demonstrated and if you have a doggie friend, let him give you a lesson, and you will have acquired the art. If the dog is difficult, and a Cairn can be difficult when he likes, you can slip him or her between your knees on the floor and then act as above. The great art of it all is to get the dog used to it all in fun without the medicine, so that when it comes to the real thing, he is not afraid.

It is usually better to give the dog medicine first thing in the morning, when the stomach is not full of undigested food, than after a heavy meal when he may get excited and disgorge everything. A dog can keep the medicine down for a long time and then throw it up, so you have to know your dog. Don't dose too much as it can do far more harm than too little, and a day's fasting won't harm any dog.

CHAPTER EIGHT

KENNELS

THIS IS THE most vexed question in the world of dogs, but is easier in the small dogs, and especially in the Cairn. If an adult house-dog, he usually knows and occupies the best chair. While I am often told this is all wrong, there will be no change for my dog. He still has his own box in the kitchen where no one can touch him, and which is cleaned out and rearranged when he is out for a walk, lest he becomes broken-hearted at seeing his old bones put into the dustbin. That is all very simple—and I have seen a bitch occupying the drawing room in a mansion house to whelp, and the window open so that she could go out and in until the pups were three weeks old, when they moved to the stable. All wrong—but then whose house and dog was it? A bitch can have a litter in the kitchen and I once visited a house up four flights where a whippet was whelping, and they were all reared there until 5 weeks old. They were dog lovers, in their own way, and everything was spot-lessly clean.

I am not advocating any of these examples but merely showing what has been done. A house-dog should be allowed out fre-quently if there is a shut-in garden, but remember that a male wan-ders more than a female. Otherwise you exercise on the lead. The music hall joke about the lamp-post, is not a joke on a wet night, but has to be faced. Hence my preference for a bitch at all times.

Happy is the owner who has an old barn or stable at hand, as the whole kennelling problem for one or many dogs is auto-matically solved. Compartments three to four feet wide and six feet deep can be formed easily and cheaply, and with a tea chest at the end with straw and a four-inch board to keep it in, the dog is safe, comfortable, and warm, and the owner has ease of mind. If straw is plentiful, a bigger division at the end, will enable the dog to dry himself with great delight after a wet ramble.

Many years ago I adopted a scheme that worked very well and

was very economical. Along a good wall, I erected a corrugated iron roof of about 30 feet length and nine feet in depth. This was supported on stout poles, and it was divided into four-foot-wide compartments. Each had a door and the whole was constructed of stout one-inch mesh. Inside was a paraffin barrel, well dried, and where vermin had not a chance of existence. At one end a round hole was cut and this faced the wall, with sufficient room for the dog to go out and in, and on the top was cut a space for the inspection of the inmates. In this run, only bitches were kept, as they rarely tried to tear the netting and they were quite able to rip wood to pieces. A good straw bedding completed the comfort, and the barrels were steadied with bricks. There was a boarding in front so that they could sit in the sun, as the run faced south, and I had no cases of chills or sickness winter or summer. They whelped in these barrels and I was fortunate in having no troublesome whelping or Caesarean operations during these years.

The kennels where the dogs were kept were of stout wood, so that no accidents could occur. I recommend having a dog and bitch together in one kennel, but not two of the same sex, and having three is asking for murder or worse some day. Dogs are just as uncertain in their tempers and their association with each other as are human beings. I was advised about this by an old Scottie breeding friend and I have never had a fight in the kennels.

It often happens that two dogs or bitches take a dislike to each other and nothing will ever make peace until they get a chance to fight it out—and my advice is to clear one of them as soon as possible, once this is apparent. It is very rare for a dog to maul a bitch, and I have only had one case personally; but the bitch does very often nip the dog.

The outdoor kennel with the chain and the dog fixed to it is something abhorrent to any right thinking person. It makes the dog savage in the end and he leads a most miserable life. To fix him up for safety for an hour or two is one thing, but regularly, is quite another. I have had a fox terrier bitch that slept in a kennel outdoors as that was the only place she had any interest in, and she was a great ratter and watch. She never wandered and while the house was all right by day—her home was the kennel at the door.

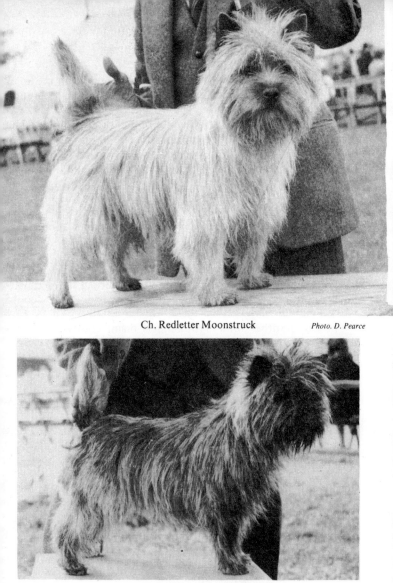

Ch. Redletter Moonstruck

Photo. D. Pearce

Ch. Redletter Moonraker

and no other dog was allowed there.

She once went a week past her whelping time and got me up at two in the morning—summer I am glad to say—as I heard a funny squeaking, and went down to see what was happening. She was lying quite happy with one all white pup suckling, and was she proud! I at once got the fire going and made my favourite drink for the whelping bitch—gruel—and how she enjoyed it!

I may say that gruel is a Scottish remedy for a cold in humans and is simply made. One handful of pinhead meal and a pinch of salt in a bowl—boiling water is poured over it and it is stirred to avoid lumps—this is allowed to settle and a lump of salt-butter put into it—it is then cooled with milk until it can be lapped up. I have never seen the bitch yet that would not lap it up and say thanks. The meal at the bottom can be used for the hens, but is not used again for the gruel. I know it is simple and old-fashioned, but I sometimes feel that in some ways we are getting too sophisticated in our dog work, and they would tell you so if they could speak.

There is one other point in the kennels, disinfection is always essential and the straw must not be allowed to be too long in changing. If not easy to get, a thick, dry sack, will make a good substitute.

Next you must attend to the whelping box and it does happen from time to time that a bitch overlies a pup, and that is a loss. A large pigbreeder once showed me how they avoid this, and it is much more common in pigs. I append a sketch of a whelping box (Figure 1), but you can make the dimensions suit your circum-

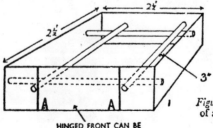

HINGED FRONT CAN BE
LET DOWN FOR CLEANING

Figure 1. A diagram of a whelping box

stances. The idea is to have a bar of wood all round the box except perhaps at the front, so that the bitch cannot squeeze into the side of the box and there is a space where the pup can lie and not get hurt. The box should be from 2 to 2½ feet square, and the bar about 3 inches from the sides. The front should hinge down for cleaning and the running of the puppies out and in when old enough. For the bars I preferred old brush handles, though many people use hollow brass tubes, but these can be cold in winter. Holes can be bored for them and pins at the end hold them in place. After the first week there is not so much chance of overlying, unless there are one or more weaklings; then the bars can be easily removed and the family have the use of the whole box. Remember that in an emergency, the ubiquitous tea chest is a very handy standby and can be got from your grocer for very little. Before use it should be disinfected in case of accidents, and being cheap it can be replaced easily. You can fit on a front flap as explained if desired, but a 4 to 6-inch board nailed up in front will save time. If the bitch is with her pups always, she gets run down and she should have a place where she can jump up and look down on the puppies, and have a little rest. I mention this for the devoted mother who at times can overdo things and give a lot of trouble in getting her into good health again. The careless one won't but even she wants a place where she can rest without being chivied by the puppies all day long—as well as all night. In cold weather this shelf should not be available by night as the dam must keep her puppies warm then. Breeding in a cold part of the world as I did, I learned this by bitter experience. Always pet the dam, and say little about the pups, as dogs can be very jealous.

CHAPTER NINE

FEEDING

To THOROUGHLY UNDERSTAND feeding, it is necessary to consider what the dog is and where he came from. In the thousands of years that have passed since he first came in contact with man, the system of feeding has changed considerably, just as with man. His teeth are that of a flesh eater, and when wild, he tears and bolts his food as quickly as possible. He swallows as much as possible as he does not know when the next meal will come along, and it is only when domesticated that he gradually changed this to a large extent. One good meal a day can keep him in condition, and if you differ on this point, pay a visit to the Zoo, and learn that the animals are fed once a day but every seventh they get nothing, which means 48 hours to rest the stomach and intestines. I have watched the carnivora at the Edinburgh Zoo, where the lions are in particularly good condition, and there is a marked contrast in the way they go for their food normally and after the 48 hours fast. Even during the war when only whale meat was available, they did not do badly, but they did not eat so voraciously. I understand that in the wild when a kill is made, the first thing to be eaten is the viscera, liver, etc, and this supplies certain vitamins not found in the lean meat, which is eaten at the end and often when it is 'high'.

With this background, it is easier to give the right food, though there is the other method which I have gone into already. We do not know the mortality in the wild very accurately, and it may be that dogs now live longer than when they were wild. I do not intend to go into a long dissertation on vitamins, as I bred and reared dogs long before the present 'high-brow' ideas, but I admit that food could be got easier and cheaper then, than at the present time.

In the small burgh in which I lived, you could buy a sheep's head, and have it singed at the local blacksmith, and better feeding could not be got. Cooked or raw it provided everything, but now you can get one skinned only, and this is just fit for cooking and making broth to soak the biscuit in. Ware bones, however, for if small pieces get into the soup they can cause severe stomach trouble. Tripe could be got then for next to nothing, and is excellent feeding, cooked or raw. Nowadays though it is not cheap. This also applies to liver.

Herring, either fresh or salt, are appreciated, as a dog does like a change just like ourselves. Bones, and the bigger the better, are excellent for supplying calcium, and help the teeth, while the gristle is a delicacy they like to tear off, cooked or raw. Then there is the standby of porridge and milk.

Any of the standard biscuits or hound meals should always be on hand, and will be taken soaked or dry, and enjoyed. Horse flesh, if you are sure that it is sound, can be given raw, but if not it should be thoroughly cooked. Then we come to the question of the household 'scraps' which are so much run down in some quarters. These help out and are enjoyed by many dogs, more than their regular food, as it is a change.

It is very difficult to deal with the 'bad' feeder and the 'picker' and you have just to consider the matter carefully and avoid trying to get him to eat. To my mind there is something wrong with him, but what it is leaves you guessing. Don't leave food lying about, and try one week of Benbow. This usually gets him to eat readily. At the same time, the daily walk should be increased so that he gets tired and his appetite encouraged. While not recommending coddling, a little raw egg and milk could be tried, but if there is no desire for food at the end of the week, and you are new to dogs, then the Vet should be consulted, although even he cannot always change a 'picker' into a good and ready eater.

I am always against trying to give a dog medicine in food—I got Gregory in jam when a child, and it took years before I looked at jam again. As I have said, I am not a believer in dosing, and while some dogs get on well with a little cod-liver oil others won't touch it. As I can't do with it myself, my sympathies are with the dog. Yeast is readily taken by most Cairns and I find that the preparation Vetzyme is very convenient, and when the pellet is rolled over the floor, it is quickly swallowed or chewed up.

WHEN TO FEED. After a big meal, a dog wants to sleep and rest, and therefore you fix the feeding hour according to circumstances. If you want the dog to be alert at night, then feed at midday, but if you live in a crowded area and want him to sleep at night and not disturb the neighbours then feed him in the evening, give him a walk out before bedtime, and everything is quiet. The Cairn even then has the ability to note every strange sound and will give warning if he thinks there is danger. If the dog is given a longish walk in the morning, he should get a biscuit, or half a large one dry when he comes in, and his ordinary meal as usual. Above everything a dog should always have access to a dish of cold water. The more flesh he eats, the more he wants to drink, and the day he gets salt herring, is the heaviest.

What I have said shouldn't be regarded as unbending laws to be followed without exception. No dog is the same and it is up to you to modify and improve on these as you study your dog. How I came to believe in salt herring, was quite accidental. I refer to the days when you had a maid and there were very, very few motor cars. We lived inland and the maid we got was a Roman Catholic and a natural dog lover and nurse. It was essential that we should have fish for Friday, and as fresh fish could not always be got, we laid in a barrel of salt herring.

Each dog in the kennel got his two days in the house for obvious reasons, and this day the bones and heads, etc., were in one plate and put on the floor to see what would happen. They disappeared at once, and so it was decided that each dog should have a salt herring on Friday together with the biscuits soaked in the boiling water of the herring. We very rarely had any sickness, and there were no left overs on that day.

Dry food helps the teeth but is often not appreciated. Where there are a number of dogs, competition helps matters a lot.

In the house, I find that a little relaxation of feeding rules helps to raise the morale of the dog. I had one that would do anything for a morsel of cheese; another that thought a bit of toast with marmalade was heaven; while a third loved that bit of toast dipped in egg. As the tail wagged and the eyes sparkled, and you felt good yourself, you knew then that you had a real companion in your Cairn and not merely a dog.

CHAPTER TEN

DOES A DOG THINK?

To MY MIND, the Cairn does think, and carefully. I at once agree that he cannot understand the difference between a murder for which you can be hanged and one that does not lead to this end— any more than the victims in either case. Reason is the prerogative of man, and I do not want to rob him of it, but I would put the Cairn on the footing of the child, and in simple matters he knows what should be done. I would regard this as thinking.

Instance: I say to a young dog, 'I don't know where your ball is, do you know?' There is no order in that and no question of being told to fetch it. He goes and finds it, knowing where he left it, and lays it at your feet. In my humble opinion there is intelligence and thinking in the way it is all done. If more work on these lines were done, I feel convinced that we would have even better friends in the Cairn Terriers.

I was running the earliest Cairn Terrier Championship show in Glasgow, and we wanted as much publicity as possible. I always work on the lines of asking for anything I need—I can only be told where to go, and after all I don't need to follow the advice. At this time the *Scottish Daily Express* was in its infancy, and I decided to ask Lord Beaverbrook for a boost in his paper. I wrote to him and nothing happened. Then one evening a very nice young gentleman called; he said he had come about this letter and what was so wonderful about a Cairn Terrier that it should be helped. I was decidedly caught on one foot, but asked him would he think it smart if he had a chocolate to hide in the room, and a dog came in and was told to seek it out, and found it no matter where it was put. He agreed, so I said all right, just a minute. He asked where the dog was and I said I had to go and borrow it.

He seemed astonished at this but I had no dogs in the house at the time, so I went to borrow Ruaridh, the most brainy Cairn that ever passed through my hands. He came out of the car, and toddled in and went to see who the stranger was, and then sat down at the fire. I explained that he visited here regularly, and made himself at home as he knew he was welcome. I then asked Mr Cole— that was and is his name I am glad to say—where he would put the chocolate when the dog was put out. He suggested under a sofa cushion, but I knew that was child's play; as soon as Ruaridh came in he would go round like a whirlwind and find it. I told Ruaridh to go out and he could find the chocolate when he came in. Behind the closed door, we considered matters and I suggested putting it on the electric light switch, but my friend did not consider this fair. I said that suited me exactly if only to prove the brains of a Cairn. When the door was opened, our friend dashed in and went round all the likely places. Then he glanced at me as much as to say, some dirty work here, and after another survey, he sat down in the middle of the room—to think, I say, and you can say what you like.

My friend said I told you, but I asked him to wait. I then explained that the Cairn was not allowed to scratch furniture and if he sat and begged below the choc, he had found it. Every particle of the air went through his nose, and then he began to move slowly towards the door—pause—more sniffing—then a quick movement to below the switch and he sat up with his paws, begging. Mr Cole handed him the choc with grace, and I got almost a quarter of the front page and a lovely group of members' dogs, free from all expense—and the public came in. A gracious help won by the brains of a Cairn for his own breed.

This dog Ruaridh in addition to having brains, was a bit of a comedian. I used to walk him along with the other dogs on a Sunday by the Canal Bank, and one day he seemed to trip over something and fall into the canal. He was duly fished out and told what he was thought of. He looked very apologetic so that no one could possibly beat him. However, the following Sunday the same thing happened at the same place, which was rather too much of a coincidence, and this time he was left to come out himself. This he duly did and stood looking as if to say 'I am a clumsy dog to fall in—I am so sorry.' But the third Sunday it was quite patent that he only wanted an excuse to get a dip, and thereafter he was on the ad a hundred yards before the 'Stumbling Block' was reached.

At his home he had about a dozen dolls, and knew every one by ame. They were kept in a waste paper basket in the kitchen, and e brought them out to play with of his own accord or when his Missus' told him which one was wanted. He never went into the ining room except on Sunday at lunch time, and then he got ome pudding in a plate. As soon as it was put on the ground he ent for one of his dolls to share it and dumped it down beside the late, while he licked it clean.

He stayed with us for a short period and went out with the other wo dogs for a walk round the block. The other two went into the itchen to see what was doing, but he continued to trot up and own the lobby, his head in the air. It was clear he was looking for omething, and then my wife remembered that on the Sunday norning he was accustomed to having a small bit of toast and acon when he came in from his walk in his own home. My wife ent and got it for him and I still smile when I remember his expression of almost pity as he looked at me while he got his toast, as the donor of the toast was the only one who understood what as right and proper.

I could recount many other tales of this odd Cairn, but my view lways was that he could think and get the best out of things, all in is own way.

CHAPTER ELEVEN

SHOW POINTS GOOD AND BAD

Handful of Cairn pups 10–12 weeks old
Note: the Black points and Dark eyes which are most desirable

I PROPOSE HERE to illustrate the main faults and good points to b
looked for in a Cairn. In Figure 2 is a good sample of a head. Not
the sharp-pointed ears, wide apart and alert. Note the eye with th
'stop' between and the length of the head equal above and belov
it, and if anything a shade longer above. Note the triangle that ca
be formed with the outside of the ears as base and the sides to th

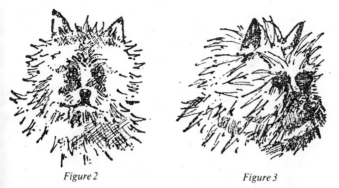

Figure 2

Figure 3

ose, and above all the expression—ready, aye ready. There is
tle fault to be found here.

In Figure 3 is a plain head with biggish ears, longer muzzle, and
top' not so good. Muzzle rather long, and balance not too good.
y comparing Figures 2 and 3, it is possible to get a fair idea of
hat is wanted.

Next we come to the front and Figure 4 is a good example. The
est must be wide so that the legs drop down straight from the

Figure 4

Figure 5

shoulders, and the feet may turn out slightly, but only slightl
This gives the dog balance and poise. The front must not t
narrow, which is the fox terrier ideal with a narrow chest ar
deep, as against the Cairn Terrier wide.

Equally important is the tail and the hindquarters and Figure
illustrates a good specimen. Firm hindquarters with well place
legs and feet, and the tail at right angle, balancing the whol
There is no over-trimming to bring it to a point which spoils mar
an outline.

CHAPTER TWELVE

SAGA OF SUSIE

IN THIS CHAPTER I propose to give the actual rearing of a puppy from three months to one year and all the thoughts and worries it brought about, and the result. Susie replaced an old dog that had been house guard and friend for years, and that had seen many pups arrive and depart, and had died eventually after an operation that was fifty-fifty. Susie arrived at 3 months after many decisions of 'Not another dog'. Her sire was a Champion and her dam went back many generations to 1912 through bitches known and owned by myself. The friend who gave her was determined that we were not to leave the breed, and we will always be indebted to her for the happiness and brightness Susie brought into the home— note I do not say 'house'.

She arrived in November a red ball of fun with two eyes that always seemed to be sizing things up. Met at the station, her box was opened in the garden as it is enclosed and there was no chance of escaping—an obvious precaution. She was very friendly and went to A., my sister-in-law, without any hesitation and then round the paths with me. She then cleaned herself, and that was the first point won, as I patted her and told her she was a very good little dog. She came right into the kitchen and had some warm milk, and then some cooked meat, as she even now is not keen on raw meat. Papers were spread all over the floor so that if accidents happened they could be put right.

Now most advisers tell you that the dog to be properly trained should have one master and one only—and they may be right. This one had two, and it loves the one and respects the other, and I was not the loved one. In the morning there was the expected puddle and it was taken out on the paper and the little dog with it, and when she cleaned herself, she was praised. From the third day onwards, except an occasional accident at night, we had no more trouble, and now she will hang on until she gets her walk outside in the morning, and leaves the garden clear.

Fortunately we found early that she was a milk lover; this was very useful and we decided to try a mixture of the American system of food always being at hand, together with a special meal from time to time. So far as health is concerned this has worked admirably. There is always a saucer of milk on the floor and a dish with a dry feed of one of the recognized manufacturers, and perhaps a sprinkling of cooked meat. She can have this when she likes and at midday a special feed as described elsewhere.

She was combed a week after arriving and did not like it and said so with her teeth. She was tapped on the nose with the comb and the combing stopped. It was resumed the following day and taken in better part, but stopped whenever she disapproved so as not to annoy her. In a week, I had only to say, what about a 'wee comb', and she would stand up to be lifted on the table, and loves it now.

I am not naturally patient but I decided with this pup not to hasten anything and see if my theory would fit into practice. No feeding between meals is urged, but this pup became part of the home and at any meal got a titbit if she asked for it—and she seldom did. A prod with her two feet meant that she was willing to try it, and this does not happen more than once or twice a week. She had her own basket in the kitchen, with her own blanket, her ball, sometimes two, and her bones. The latter would be thinned out when she went round the garden with me or for walks later on, and she always noted what had happened and looked rather disturbed.

Then came the lead and it was here the dual control did not work well. She resented the collar and sulked all day and A. took it off, and all was well. Two or three days afterwards it was tried again, and the resentment was not so strong, and in less than a week it was suffered in silence and not looked on as a sign of being in disgrace; but this gradually passed away, and by five months she forgot all about it.

I never put a lead on a dog until it is six months old, rightly or wrongly, and when I first put the lead on Susie she was very annoyed and pulled and struggled. However, I took her round the

arden, and then let her off. The lead was hung near her basket so
hat she could see it, and then she was told to get her collar on (the
ead) and be taken out. Once or twice a day this went on, and in
hree days she would walk in a sort of way, but not willingly. One
norning she was not taken out, and A. told me that the pup had
)een jumping up to the lead and collar, and so I knew another step
ıad been won. In late afternoon I asked her would she put her
ollar on and she shot into her basket and stood up. Remember
hat up to this time she had never been allowed outside the garden,
hough three times she had dodged out and had to be followed up
ınd carried home. Like many another she wanted to see what was
)n the other side of the wall.

Her first walk out and into the wood was a pull devil pull baker,
)ut within a week she was quite controlled and when let loose in
he wood, she returned when called to get her collar on. There
ıever was much trouble about the collar once this was under-
tood, and she tries to understand. No definite words of command
ıave ever been used but just conversation and change of voice.

At four months she had her first car ride and did not like it—
ather scared, and wanted to be in a corner—but it passed away
apidly, and now she loves it and it is not safe to use the word 'car'
n the house, or the word 'walk', if you want to avoid hilarious
greement in her understanding the words. We can still spell with
afety, but she is so cute, that I doubt if that will always pass
nuster. There is a routine which she understands quite well—
valk in forenoon—rest in afternoon in her own basket, but in the
neantime she has acquired certain rights and she sees she gets
hem.

Thoroughly spoiled did you say—I believe you—but so lovable
ınd loving that I think she is better that way. She loves her missus
ınd at four o'clock reports for anything that is going in the sweet
ıne, and mayhap a little tea. Anything that you eat is good enough
or her she says, even when it comes to pieces of orange or apple.

Her routine is very definite. She knows she must go out the first
hing in the morning, when the three ducks are let out and she
amples their water. Then into the house to find her missus, and
hey 'spin the tale to each other'. When I appear on the scene she

wants her ball which is soft rubber, $2\frac{1}{4}$ inches in diameter, her constant plaything since she arrived. We never know where it was left last and look for it, and when we give up, she shortly afterwards puts it at her missus' feet, to help two deluded individuals. It is bounced for her for a little and then she takes it to her basket to chew. It is never wanted again until the following morning, unless we have a caller whom she specially likes, and then it is brought out so that it may be bounced a bit.

During the day she sits at the fence and knows everyone who goes up and down and they know her, and looking at her it is obvious how proud she is of all the attention she gets. After lunch she waits until her missus sits down and then on to the chair like a streak of lightning, nose into side pocket, and the handkerchief is gone. The two of them then have a long argument about this bit of fun, the article is recovered and she retires to her basket until 4 p.m.

I usually get a cup of milk at night, to wash a pill down, and one night when the pup looked a bit down in the mouth, I gave her some of the warm milk in the saucer. That is now a fixed custom and she won't go to bed until I get the milk and she gets her small share, and then of her own accord she goes to her basket and peace reigns until the morning.

She has no fear and no nerves. She loves children, and goes up to the biggest dog with her tail wagging. There have been no troubles yet, and as she went along, she matured and learned. On the lead, if she pulls, I merely say 'Steady no pulling', and it stops but she is less reasonable going out than coming home, after she has galloped up hill and down dale. She is full of the joy of life and makes the years drop from one's shoulders.

She used to help me to dress in her way, by pulling my socks etc, down to the bathroom, but that stage has passed. She always pinched a pair of old slippers as soon as I took them off and (as all thinking people will know) the older they became the more valuable. She was forever running off with them and I decided to let her have them. They are both in her box and in the afternoon or evening when she feels in good form, each slipper in turn is tossed in the air and pulled round the room and generally treated like the ball, except that when tired of it, she tucks them in below her in her basket.

I use two tones of voice for her, one when she is doing right and the short harsh one when I want something done. Whenever she hears the harsh 'Steady' she stands and waits; but when I come in and ask 'Where is my wee doggie' she dashes up to say 'Here she is'. She is not perfect and there is a long way to go yet, but the start has been made and she understands talk. She has been developed like a child, and we look forward to many happy years of comradeship. There will be storms no doubt and gloomy weather, as in life, but it is worth it all. So if you want to have a 'spoiled dog', I have shown you how to train it, but you will find at the end of the day that you have a friend whose cold nose will always be in your hand and whose devotion will never waver no matter how the world treats you. When you read of Bill Sykes and his dog, you will realize that Dickens did know something about the best friend of man; but never for a moment believe that

> A woman, a dog, and a walnut tree,
> The more you lick them the better they be.

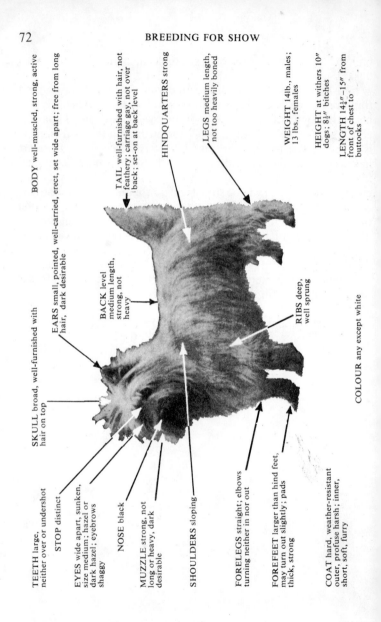

BODY well-muscled, strong, active; free from long

TAIL well-furnished with hair, not feathery; carriage gay, not over back; set-on at back level

HINDQUARTERS strong

LEGS medium length, not too heavily boned

WEIGHT 14lb., males; 13 lbs., females

HEIGHT at withers 10" dogs; 8½" bitches

LENGTH 14¼"–15" from front of chest to buttocks

SKULL broad, well-furnished with hair on top

EARS small, pointed, well-carried, erect, set wide apart; free from long hair, dark desirable

BACK level medium length, strong, not heavy

RIBS deep, well sprung

TEETH large, neither over or undershot

STOP distinct

EYES wide apart, sunken, size medium; hazel or dark hazel; eyebrows shaggy

NOSE black

MUZZLE strong, not long or heavy, dark desirable

SHOULDERS sloping

FORELEGS straight; elbows turning neither in nor out

FOREFEET larger than hind feet, may turn out slightly; pads thick, strong

COLOUR any except white

COAT hard, weather-resistant outer, profuse harsh; inner, short, soft, furry

CHAPTER THIRTEEN

BREEDING FOR SHOW

THIS IS A very debatable subject, and I have no intention of laying
own the law about it, but discussing it, with one example given,
nd my opinion of the best stud dog.

At a show you hear a lot of talk about 'families' and 'lines' and
nbreeding and outbreeding, with this stud dog recommended as
ure to get winners. There are one or two points that are over-
ooked in this matter, and the most serious is that some people
orget that a pup has two parents—a sire and a dam and there is
ne influence of both to be considered. My view is that the owner
vith the bitches is the breeder in the stronger position as he can
ick his stud dogs, whereas the stud dog owner can't pick his
itches.

Then a bitch usually does not produce more than two litters in
ne year—say 10 puppies—and if she has one or two winners that
 quite good, say an average of 25 per cent. In the same period the
tud dog produces dozens of litters, and the percentage of winners
 surprisingly low when you work it out. Of course, you can prove
nything by figures.

My advice is to get a good bitch or a well-bred bitch pup, which
hould be as near your ideal as possible. When you see a winner,
ry to see the sire and dam if possible—you learn a lot this way.
tudy the pedigree very carefully as it may merely be a string of
ames with the champions in red ink, without any one dog or
itch appearing more than once or twice, and this will get you
owhere. There should appear some pattern to show that the
reeder of your stock bitch had some idea of inbreeding to Ch
nooks, a male, or Ch Miss Pert, a female. This concentrates good
r bad points, and you try to carry on in the same lines. Now we
ome to the more difficult point.

When the lines and families were taken up it was for race horses,
nd may have proved a valuable asset there (I am no judge). It will

73

be kept in mind that race horses are valued for their speed, stam ina, and strength, but in the dog show it is appearance or shall say beauty. It does not matter whether the winner of the Derby i big or little, and if he wins the triple crown you can expect him t have all the racing virtues, and whether he was spotted like a leo pard or had no mane or tail, does not matter so far as the purpos for which he was wanted matters.

It is not so with the dog when it is all outward appearance tha counts, and the more you know of your breed's outward appear ance, the more hope there is of your producing a champion. If yo know a certain dog has a splendid movement, see then if he has ex pression. If good limbs, then see can he use them, and with thes details you soon know where your stock is deficient and can wor out a plan to get over it by inbreeding or even outbreeding.

Don't worry about Telegony—that is the influence of a pre vious sire on future stock—it is a myth. If, however, you fin someone who believes in it and is willing to make a present of th bitch to you, and she happens to be a good one, or who is willin to take a quarter of the value, don't let him or her out of your sigh until you have completed the deal and your collar is on the bitch. never met one of this kind in all the years, who would throw bitch away although he alleged she was 'spoiled'.

You never know how a pup is going to turn out and in a recen straw poll of all the dog breeds of America, the 'picker' in eac breed was said to be an expert. There are over a couple of hundre breeds in America and, please don't laugh, there were over couple of hundred ways and times of picking. According to on toy expert, you picked it when it was born, but two others said th first and the other the last born. This was the earliest possible c course. The last picker was at three days short of the year, and was a big breed, which would be slow in maturing; but still decision should be made before that time, in my view.

So it is clear that you have as much hope of picking a winner you have risk of selling the best. The bonnie baby in the crad may turn out in the end to look like a film gangster, and vice vers You know that is true and there is no reason why it should n apply to dogs also. So long as there are no definite faults such curled tails or very light eyes, the healthy lively puppy that comes to you at once, is the most promising, but study the weakling as he can pick up. I saw the breeder of a crack litter keep the 'best', but the buyer, and I agreed with her, thought otherwise, and this was the opinion of the judges later, so you see it is all a gamble. If the reader ever finds a sure way of picking the best, let me know and we can make a fortune between us.

PARTICULAR CASE OF BREEDING. It is often said that you can get to the top of the tree in any breed if you have money. To some extent this is true, as you can buy in, getting the best. Winning then becomes routine. But the best way is to breed in, and on the accompanying pedigree I wish to show how it can be done, of course with a little luck, but without being a millionaire.

The first time you would note the prefix Fincairn, is in the K.C. Stud book of 1947, and the first postwar shows started in 1946. It presumably had been passed by the K.C. in the latter year. In November the same year there appeared at the Cairn Terrier Club Show a bitch named Fincairn Graegirl, who appeared for many a year in the Cairn pedigrees. She made no splash but looked a good type and came from two well-known Scottish kennels. The sire was Beechacre Bomber, and this prefix went back to the first war, while the dam was Mareg of Fair City who traced back in one kennel to the same time. In other words you knew what was there, good, bad, or indifferent, and this knowledge is the most valuable asset in breeding.

It was decided to mate her to Ch Valiant Rob Roy of Rhosbridge, who was the first post war champion, and in whose pedigree appeared a wonderful bitch named Ch Shinnel Wistful. From the mating came a bitch Fincairn Jennifer, who appeared in November 1948, and won the Beechacre Cup for the best bitch puppy, a rather interesting win. She was a decided improvement on her dam from a show point of view and held out great promise for breeding. The problem was what sire.

At this time there was a Champion sired by Rob Roy and whose dam Bunty of Brackendene was also suitable for breeding to Jennifer. The result was Gillian whelped on 10th February 1949, and

PEDIGREE OF CHAMPION FINCAIRN GILLIAN

Ch Fincairn Gillian

- **Sire Ch Brackendene Brig of Cona Lynn**
  - Ch Valiant Rob Roy of Rhosbridge
    - Valiant Drummer
      - Beechacre Bugler.
      - Ch Prinelo Lady Jester.
    - Rhosbridge Rosalind
      - Stonecracker of Pledwick.
      - Ch Shinnel Wistful.
  - Bunty of Brackendene
    - Foxglove Warrior
      - Furzefield Chimpet.
      - Wonder Lass.
    - Rhosbridge Rebecca
      - Domino of Darwencote.
      - Barbara of Brackendene
- **Fincairn Jennifer**
  - Ch Valiant Rob Roy of Rhosbridge
    - Valiant Drummer
      - Beechacre Bugler.
      - Ch Princelo Lady Jester.
    - Rhosbridge Rosalind
      - Stonecracker of Pledwick,
      - Ch Shinnel Wistful.
  - Fincairn Graegirl
    - Beechacre Bomber
      - Beechacre Baron
      - Beechacre Bunting.
    - Mareg of Fair City
      - Malva of Fair City.
      - Fan of Fair City.

Note specially where the concentration or inbreeding comes in and the breeding back.

  Inbred to Ch Rob Roy is the usual term.

whose first championship show was in Edinburgh, 1950, where she won 2nd Limit and 1st Open, going on to the Kensington Canine in London later in the year and getting her first certificate. Her last certificate was won in Glasgow in the spring of 1955, and she was retired from the ring. A wonderful record for a small kennel, and more so when it was stated that she has bred Champions of both sexes that are carrying on her good points. My own special interest is that she was so like Ch Shinnel Wistful, whom I admired so much in the years before the war.

The owner of this bitch placed Gillian third once in a class with three champions, and recognized the strong resemblance when it was pointed out to her at the end of the show. I give the pedigree in full opposite, and it is worth studying by those who want to get to the top, and intend to breed carefully against the big kennels and to beat them. It can be done, and here is the instance.

CHAPTER FOURTEEN

CLUBS

THE LEADING AUTHORITY in the Dog World is the Kennel Club and their address is 1/4 Clarges Street, Piccadilly, London, W.1.

In the Cairn Terrier Breed the senior club is The Cairn Terrier Club, and the present secretary is Mr. T. A. Hogg, 34 Telford Road, Edinburgh EH4. The Secretary of this club must reside in Scotland, but of course the official and the address may change in any of the clubs.

Then comes the Southern Cairn Terrier Club, with the present Secretary, Mr F. Edwards, The Sanctuary Annex, Steeple Ashton, Trowbridge, Wilts.

The Cairn Terrier Association, comes next with Mrs B. Dewhurst, Whinney Hill House, Altham, Accrington, Lancs, as Secretary and Treasurer.

Any of these clubs will help the beginner, and this also applies to the members of the various clubs. Each one has a badge which can be recognized at once, and is a sure sign of a lover of the 'the Best Little Pal in the World'.

There are also Cairn Terrier Clubs on the Continent and the U.S.A., as well as throughout the Commonwealth.